INSPIRING STORIES
FOR AMAZING BOYS

Amelia Kinsley

Content

Introduction

Hey! It's wonderful that you have taken the time to read this book. I'm sure you're already curious about what's in store for you. But first, I want to tell you a secret. It's a very important secret that can accompany you throughout your life. So, pay close attention and read the following lines carefully.

Do you know that you are very special? Although there are millions of boys and girls

in this world, there is only one of you.
No one is exactly like you. You are
completely unique, and you should always
remember that. When life becomes difficult,
you must always remember that you are
unique and important to this world just the
way you are.

Sometimes, life is not easy; there are many
small and big challenges in our lives.
Every obstacle requires self-awareness,
courage, and self-confidence.
Sometimes, you may think you can't solve a
problem. Maybe you will even feel terrified
and doubt yourself. The truth is: everyone
feels this way from time to time—even
adults!

Yes, you heard that right. Mom, Dad,
Grandma, Grandpa, and even your teachers

sometimes lack courage and confidence. So, be brave, don't give up, and never lose faith in yourself.

Every day is full of surprises. There are many wonderful days you probably wish would never end. Sooner or later, everyone will experience days when not everything goes according to plan. Things will happen that make us very sad, scared, or even angry. These bad days are also a part of life. There can be no joy in life without some bad experiences. Without the bad, we can't fully appreciate the good.

This book has many stories where you will meet wonderful boys. Boys who overcome their fears. Boys who are brave. Boys who show inner strength. You can do all of this too. You must believe in yourself.

I hope these stories help you do so.
In the following pages, small and big dreams
come true.

P.S. After each story, you will find a mandala
with a special message. You can color the
mandala, especially with many different
bright colors. Take your time and enjoy the
process. Coloring the mandala will help you
remember the message better.

Have fun reading!

Ben and the Squirrel

The alarm clock rang and pulled Ben out of a deep dream. He yawned loudly and sleepily rubbed his eyes. Ben was a cheerful boy with short brown hair.
He had turned eight last week and was in the second grade.

Ben stretched and wiggled a bit in bed, then slowly stood up. He went to the window of his room and carefully pushed aside the yellow curtains. Then, he opened the window. It was seven in the morning, and the first rays of the sun lit up the room. The fresh morning air flowed toward him.

He took a deep breath and looked out the window at the big trees and the many flowers that bloomed on the lawn. It was a beautiful morning, but Ben still didn't feel well that day. He loved warm summer days. Usually, he couldn't wait to run outside to soak up the sunshine in the backyard. But today, he preferred to stay inside.

Ben wandered restlessly around his room for a while. Finally, he made up his mind, put on his favorite blue shirt, and made his bed. He also packed his bag with notebooks and books to prepare for school.

Ben also didn't forget to take his gym bag. Crammed inside the bag were track pants, a T-shirt, and tennis shoes. On Fridays, he had gym class during the last hour.

Usually, Ben loved this hour, but today everything was completely different.

Last week, Ben's teacher, Mrs. Peterson, announced they would use the climbing rope in the next gym class. Ben felt terrified. He had never climbed anywhere in his life. With a lump in his throat, he thought about his classmates. If he failed, they might laugh at him or even call him mean names. Hundreds of thoughts raced through Ben's head, and he felt dizzy.

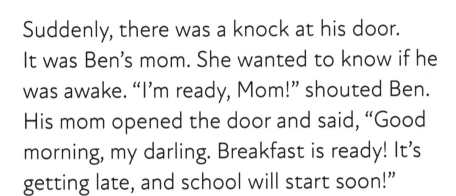

Suddenly, there was a knock at his door. It was Ben's mom. She wanted to know if he was awake. "I'm ready, Mom!" shouted Ben. His mom opened the door and said, "Good morning, my darling. Breakfast is ready! It's getting late, and school will start soon!"

"Just a minute!" replied Ben. He swung his bag onto his back and reached for his gym bag with his right hand.

As he was about to close the window in his room, Ben heard a loud rustling sound outside. Curious, he looked where the noise was coming from. That's when he saw it! A small, reddish-brown squirrel was nimbly climbing a large tree in the backyard. Hurriedly, it reached the top of the tree.

"Oh, if only I could climb as well as you

do, little squirrel. Then, the climbing rope would be easy for me, and I wouldn't have to be afraid anymore ..." Ben sighed softly to himself.

With a frown, he closed the window and made his way to the kitchen.

Mom had already prepared breakfast there. There were fresh rolls with delicious strawberry jam and hot chocolate to drink. Dad was already sitting at the table, happily drinking his coffee while he read the newspaper.

Ben was not hungry, because he felt anxious.

However, Mom always said it was important not to leave the house without eating breakfast. So, with a heavy heart, Ben ate a small roll covered with jam. After all, he didn't want to feel hungry during class. "So, what's on the agenda for school today?" asked Dad.

Ben quickly swallowed his last bite and answered, "First I have math, then English, and finally gym class!"

For a moment, Ben thought he might tell his parents about his fear of the climbing rope. He decided against it.

Somehow, he didn't want to talk to Mom and Dad about it now, although he usually talked everything over with them.
After breakfast, he ran to the bathroom,

carefully brushed his teeth, and combed his hair with the brush. Then he said goodbye to his parents, who gave him a kiss on the forehead and wished him a good day at school.

Ben made his way to the bus. The bus stop was only a few minutes from Ben's house. He heard a rustling sound again. Then, he saw the squirrel from before. It had a nut in its hands and was only a few feet away from Ben. The squirrel also noticed the boy. It stood on its hind legs and gazed deeply into Ben's eyes. "You're not going to take my nut, are

you?" the squirrel asked cheekily.

Ben stood in front of the cute animal with his jaw on the floor and his eyes wide. He was unable to believe what was happening. Did the squirrel really speak to him, or was he dreaming?

"You ... you ... you can talk?" stuttered Ben in disbelief.

"Yes, I can, but I rarely actually talk to people. For you, today, I'll make an exception, dear Ben, because I like you!" replied the squirrel.

"Hh...Hh...how do you know my name?" asked Ben in complete amazement.

"Well, we're neighbors! I've been living on that birch tree over there for some time. From there, I sometimes watch you play with your friends or talk to your parents. That's how I learned your name.

Where are my manners? My name is Frederik, but you can call me Fred. Tell me, you kids have to go to school in the morning, right? I think you need to leave soon!" said the squirrel.

"Hello, Fred. It's nice to meet you!" Ben replied with a smile. Then, he continued with a slightly hushed and more serious tone, "Well, actually, I don't want to go to school today. I'm supposed to climb the climbing rope in gym class, and I'm terrified of it." "But, Ben, you don't have to be scared of that at all. Take a deep breath and don't look down. You'll find that it's not that hard!" said Fred, smiling and nodding his tiny head to try to cheer Ben up.

"Well, that's easy for you to say. After all, you're a squirrel and you're naturally great

at climbing. But, Fred, I can't!" sighed Ben in frustration. Fred felt sorry for the little boy. He scratched his head with his right hand and pondered about how he could help Ben.

Then he started to say:
"Yes, you are absolutely right. Today, I can climb really well, but, you know, I wasn't like that from the start.
I remember when I was a little baby squirrel. The first time I had to climb a tree by myself, I was as scared as you are now.
Honestly, it's okay to feel scared and nervous about new things, but you shouldn't let it stop you.

If you really want to climb that rope, then you have to believe in yourself.
I, for one, believe in you. You can do it!"

Ben listened intently to Fred. While listening, he discovered a new, overwhelming sense of courage. Fred was right. He could do it if he believed in himself. He would have liked to chat with him some more, but now he really had to hurry to school.

"Thank you for your help, Fred. I will remember what you said. You helped me a lot. I hope to see you again soon."
Hastily, he waved to Fred. Fred had already dashed back up the tree trunk. He glanced briefly at Ben, and then he disappeared into the dense branches. With renewed courage to face life, Ben got on the bus and went to school. He decided to face his fear.

"Brrrring!" rang the school bell. The time had finally come for Ben to climb the dreaded climbing rope. Ben could hardly concentrate on his classwork that morning. He couldn't stop thinking about Fred and his words.

It was 11 o'clock, and it was time for his gym class to begin. The children walked with their teacher, Mrs. Peterson, to the gymnasium, which was right next to the school building. After everyone had changed into their gym clothes, they gathered in front of the climbing rope. Mrs. Peterson said to the children, "As we discussed last week, we are going to climb the climbing rope."

Before they started climbing, everyone had to do warm-up exercises. Then, they lined up. One by one, they climbed the rope. Some climbed quickly and skillfully, but others climbed slowly and carefully. Ben's heart began to beat faster and faster. He gazed reluctantly at the long rope he needed to master. To prevent injuries, soft blue mats lay on the floor in front of them. This calmed Ben down a bit, but he still felt nervous. The rope was not particularly high, but to Ben, it seemed like Mount Everest. He stood at the very back of the line so he could watch the other children conquer the rope first. Ben realized many of the other children also seemed anxious.

Then, it was his turn. Immediately, his heart began to pound out of his chest, but he couldn't give up now. Not under any circumstances. He had to, at least, try to do his best. He thought again about Fred's words and finally walked toward the rope. Ben closed his eyes for a moment and took another deep breath. Then, he began to climb. The first part was difficult, and his feet trembled a little bit. Nevertheless, with each pull and push, it felt easier and easier. Ben continued to climb. With excitement, he wondered how high he had climbed. He was curious and tried to catch a glimpse, but then he remembered Fred's advice: Don't look down!

He paused briefly and gathered his strength again. He went a bit farther and finally reached the top. After a short pause, he carefully climbed down until he felt his feet touch the ground again.
He made it!

A feeling of joy and pride rose within him. A big grin lit up his face as he beamed with pride and happiness.

"That was great how you climbed to the top, Ben. Almost as graceful as a squirrel!" Mrs. Peterson praised the boy and winked at him as if she knew about his mentor, the squirrel.

After gym class, Ben headed home with John. He would have loved to tell John the story of his new furry friend, but Ben kept his special little secret. Still, Ben seemed to be in a daydream.
He skipped the rest of the way home, thinking over and over about how he mastered the climbing rope. He felt free and overjoyed. Once he arrived home, Ben couldn't wait to tell Fred. He had to be the

first to know. So, he ran into the backyard and stopped right under the birch tree.

"Fred, where are you?" the boy called, looking around in all directions. Again and again, he called out as loud as he could, and he didn't care if anyone heard him. He had to tell him.

Suddenly, Fred came running. His bushy tail wagged back and forth. He stood in front of Ben, looking at him questioningly.
"Fred, there you are at last! You won't believe it! I climbed all the way to the top. I could never have done it without your advice. Thanks for your help!" Ben said, beaming with joy. He wanted to take the cute little animal in his arms. Fred reared back a little and replied, "You're welcome, but you have only yourself to thank for that.

After all, you were the one climbing that rope, not me. I was just giving you advice. I was convinced you would make it. I am also quite sure that you will achieve so much more in your life.

You must simply believe in yourself. Now, I must continue collecting nuts and seeds for the winter. Goodbye and see you soon."

Ben wanted to talk more with Fred. But, before he knew it, Fred gracefully climbed another tree and disappeared behind the branches and leaves.

It took Ben a moment to understand his new friend's words. He still felt as if he were caught in a beautiful dream.
Fred was right. He climbed alone, and he had done it because he conquered his fear. Still, Fred was a great help to him, and, for that, he felt grateful. With a smile, Ben looked up at the tree once more, hoping to catch a glimpse of Fred. However, Fred had already jumped to another tree and was busy looking for supplies for the winter.

Today, Ben learned he could do more by himself than he initially thought. So much was possible if he only believed in himself.

Who knows? Maybe Ben would become a mountaineer and climb Mount Everest?

Whatever his life might be in the future, he would never forget this day.

Thank you, Fred!

I am proud of myself !

The Test of Courage

Do you know what a dare is? Maybe you've heard about it at some point. In a dare, you are supposed to do something and overcome your fear. For example, letting a spider crawl on your hand, touching a stinging nettle, or even eating an earthworm. Yuck! This story is about a similar dare.

Lucas was ten years old and in the fourth grade. He was an extremely cheerful boy. At school, he had two very good friends. Their names were Brandon and Tyler, and they were in the same class as Lucas. The three boys liked to meet after school, and they spent a lot of time together. They did their homework together, played card games, and goofed around. Today, once again, they met at Lucas' home.

After playing Uno in the apartment for an hour, they decided to go outside. It was a mid-August afternoon, and it was pleasantly warm. Only a few small clouds covered the bright sun. Birds chirped merrily from the trees.

Lucas lived with his parents outside the city in a rural area with many trees, bushes, and meadows full of flowers. Occasionally, sheep and cows grazed in the meadows. For a few weeks, the three boys had been challenging each other with dares when alone in nature. Brandon and Tyler came

up with wild ideas. Lucas, by contrast, was not fond of most of the dares. However, he didn't dare to tell his friends. After all, he didn't want to be called a chicken or seem like a downer. That's why Lucas had participated in every dare.

As the boys walked past a tall walnut tree, Brandon once again had an idea for a new dare.

Full of enthusiasm, Brandon said to Lucas and Tyler: "I just thought of a dare. See that big tree over there? Which one of you dares to climb up there?"

Lucas gulped. He frowned thoughtfully. Climbing such a tall tree was not something he was comfortable with. He gathered all his courage and decided to speak his mind,

"Well, I don't think that's a good idea. If you fell from that height, you could break every bone in your body! There's no way I'm going to climb up there, and I hope you guys don't either! Climbing a tree that tall is way too risky!" For the very first time, Lucas spoke up about how he really felt.

"Are you scared?" asked Brandon with a mischievous grin. "You sound like a scaredy-cat! Lucas is a scaredy-cat!" exclaimed Tyler in a loud voice.

For Lucas, it hurt that Brandon and Tyler were making fun of him. He still stuck to his decision not to climb the tree. It was simply way too dangerous.

Brandon now went to the tree and said confidently, "All right. Then, I'll show the

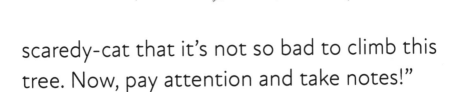

scaredy-cat that it's not so bad to climb this tree. Now, pay attention and take notes!"

Then, Brandon began to climb. Branch by branch, he pulled himself higher and higher. With every step he took, the branches cracked, and they grew thinner the further up he climbed. Broken branches fell to the ground. When Brandon reached the halfway point, he climbed onto a thicker branch to take a short break. From there, he looked down at Lucas and Tyler.
"Look at how high I am! I told you there's nothing to be afraid of. This is totally easy!" cheered Brandon.
But then it suddenly happened!
Out of sheer joy, Brandon relaxed for a moment, and he lost his balance. With all his might, he tried to hold on to a branch, but it was too late.

He fell from the tree and landed on the ground with a big thump.

"Ouch!" moaned Brandon in pain. He had fallen directly on his right thigh. Immediately, Lucas and Tyler ran to help him.
"Are you all right? Are you in pain?" asked Lucas worriedly.
"I think I broke my leg. Also, I feel so dizzy. I need a doctor. Help me, please!" sobbed Brandon with tears running down his face. Lucas didn't hesitate for a moment and ran home as fast as he could.

He frantically told his mother about what happened to Brandon. Lucas' mother dialed

911 and called for help. Then, Lucas ran back to the scene of the accident as quickly as his little legs could carry him. He wanted to wait for the ambulance with Brandon and Tyler.

About ten minutes later, the paramedics arrived. One paramedic was wearing a yellow and red uniform and carried an emergency medical pack with him so he could examine Brandon closely. He carefully palpated his leg and then said, "I think it would be best to X-ray your leg at the hospital."
Using a blue, ice-cold plastic bag, he cooled the injured leg to reduce the swelling.
Brandon was carefully carried into the ambulance and driven to the hospital.
Tyler and Lucas accompanied him to offer their support.

While the three boys waited for the X-ray, Brandon said to Lucas, "You were right. This was a stupid dare. I should have listened to you, but instead, I laughed at you.

I'm so sorry! Thank you for calling an ambulance for me so quickly. You are a really great friend!" Tyler also apologized to Lucas, "I'm also sorry for calling you a scaredy-cat earlier. That was mean of me, and it was not okay."

"It's okay. We all make mistakes sometimes. Besides, we're best friends after all! Apology accepted!" replied Lucas with a reassuring smile on his face.

Now, the doctor came back. He held a large X-ray in his hand, showing Brandon's thigh.

"You're lucky, Brandon. You bruised your leg badly, but it's not broken! You have to rest your leg for a while and apply a special ointment. In two to three weeks, your leg should be fully recovered. Just don't do any more dangerous things," the doctor warned.

Immediately, the three boys breathed a sigh of relief. Thank goodness nothing worse had happened to Brandon.

Lucas was glad he listened to his heart. Courage means daring to do something, but safety and assessing whether something might be too dangerous is also important. You don't always have to play the superhero to show courage.

It also shows courage to say "no" when you don't want to do something.

Sometimes, you show more courage by saying "no" than by being brave and doing something dangerous. Lucas showed true courage and bravery by speaking his mind and standing up for what he believed in.

I trust myself!

A Bad Day

Noah sat nervously in his seat. He glanced at the door. Soon, Mr. Smith would come into the classroom and start the English lesson. Frantically, he drew a sunflower in his sketchbook. Noah always drew when he felt anxious. The process helped distract him, but today, it wasn't working. His stress was too great.

Noah sat next to his friend James. The two had met in kindergarten and become good friends. Now, they were in the same class and sat next to each other.

Noah said to James, "Today, we'll get our grades from last week's test. I don't have a good feeling. I made a lot of mistakes, and the test was pretty hard."

Unlike Noah, James didn't seem anxious. James always got straight A's in English and probably expected a very good grade on this test. James looked at Noah with a surprised expression and said, "Well, I thought the test was pretty easy!"

That was exactly what Noah didn't want to hear right now. Still, he would be happy for his friend if he got an A again. Secretly, Noah wished James had agreed the test wasn't easy.

With long strides, Mr. Smith entered the classroom. He placed his large brown briefcase on the desk. Then, he greeted the students in a cheery mood, "What a wonderful morning! I've finally corrected last week's test. I'm sure you're all eager to see what grades you've received."

A loud murmur passed through the classroom. It seemed Noah wasn't the only one who would rather not find out what he scored on his test.

Some students whispered frantically. Others stared silently at the floor, playing with their pencil cases or biting their fingernails.

Mr. Smith took a stack of papers out of his folder. As if under a spell, the students paid close attention to every word Mr. Smith said,

"There is only one A, four B's, eight C's, two D's, and, unfortunately, an F!"

Noah's stomach dropped. He felt sick at the thought that he might have gotten the F. His face turned ghostly white. He definitely didn't want to have the only F, but now he feared the worst.

Mr. Smith began to go through the rows from front to back, personally handing the test grades to each student. Noah and James sat together at a table in the third row.

It took a while for Mr. Smith to reach their table. For Noah, it felt like half an eternity, and he became more anxious as the seconds ticked by. First, Mr. Smith gave James his test grade. He held James' test in his hands, looked at the grade, and then said with a

smile, "Very nicely done, James! You got the highest score! You didn't make a single mistake! Keep it up!"

Then, he happily laid the test on the table in front of James. Once again, he had earned an A. "Yay!" exclaimed James with joy, and he beamed from ear to ear. Mr. Smith was also obviously in a good mood and was happy for his star student.

Now, Mr. Smith began to look in the pile of papers for Noah's test. When he found it, his mood became more serious. Mr. Smith placed the test on the table in front of Noah and bent down to him.

"I actually expected a better performance from you. What happened?" Mr. Smith whispered in Noah's ear so that the other students couldn't hear him. Noah looked at the red F on his test and swallowed.

"I... I... I don't know exactly what happened..." Noah whispered back softly.

"Well, then, I guess you had a bad day. It can happen to anyone! I'm sure you'll do better next time!" said Mr. Smith quietly. Then he stood upright again and went to the next student.

Noah looked at his test as if it was a venomous spider. Almost every sentence had a mistake marked by Mr. Smith. He started to tear up. He didn't want to cry in front of his classmates, so he held back his tears and tried not to let any emotions show. He had never felt so sad in his entire life.

Fortunately, class was over soon. Noah couldn't wait to finally be alone in his room.

On the way home, Noah thought about what he should tell his parents. Noah was ashamed he had made the worst grade. That's why he didn't want to mention the test. He quickly realized that wouldn't

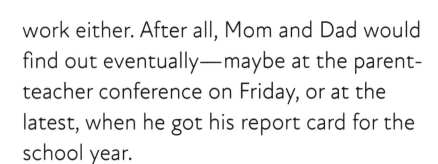

work either. After all, Mom and Dad would find out eventually—maybe at the parent-teacher conference on Friday, or at the latest, when he got his report card for the school year.

Noah arrived home discouraged. Dad was still at work until 2:00 p.m., but Mom was already home and had made lunch for the family.

"Hello, Noah! I'm glad you're here. I made us spaghetti. We'll have applesauce for dessert. Let's eat right away while it's still warm! Dad's going to be a little late coming home from work today!" Mom said warmly and gave Noah a kiss on the forehead.
Although Noah had little appetite, he sat down at the table with his mother. It didn't take long for Mom to notice Noah's sadness.

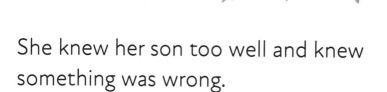

She knew her son too well and knew something was wrong.

"What's the matter, sweetie? Why are you so quiet today?" she asked. Noah just shrugged his shoulders and remained silent. "You know you can tell me anything that's on your mind, right? I'm your mother, after all! Did anything bad happen at school?" Mom asked, stroking Noah's cheek lovingly.

Finally, Noah found his words and answered with tears in his eyes, "Yes, I got an F on my test! I don't know how that could have happened. I studied enough, but it was just too hard for me." Tears now began to stream down Noah's cheeks. Mom hugged him tightly to comfort him.

After Noah calmed down, Mom began to say, "Although you probably see it differently right now, I don't think a bad grade is the end of the world. And it's nothing to be ashamed of. You did your best, and that's what really counts. I once got an F in school and was very sad, but failures are also part of life.

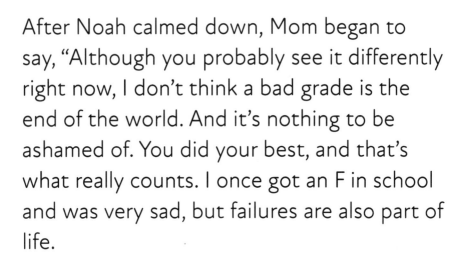

Everything can't always go perfectly, even if we want it to. You will certainly have the opportunity to improve your overall grade. It's not bad, my darling!"

"Yes, it is bad!" Noah contradicted, completely upset.

"After all, you have to do well in school so you can get a good job later on. Besides, I'm annoyed that James always gets A's. He's always better than me! Why can't I be as smart as he is?"

Mom replied softly, "A grade doesn't say anything about what you can accomplish in your life. If you have a dream, then the most important thing is to believe in yourself.

I will always love you no matter what grades you get. You are a wonderful boy. No grade in the world can change how much I love you because grades don't determine a person's worth!"

It took a little while for Noah to really understand what Mom had told him. Then, he wiped the tears from his face, took a

deep breath, and said, "I love you too, Mom." Noah was glad to have such a great mom. He was relieved Mom didn't mind that he hadn't done well on the test.

In the afternoon, Dad finally came home from work. He told Noah he had often earned a bad grade and wasn't the best student. However, he has a job that makes him happy.

Mom and Dad were proud Noah was so brave and open with them about his fears. From now on, Noah promised himself never to feel devastated by a bad grade again.

After all, there are much more important things in life. As Mom said so beautifully at lunch: a grade does not determine the value of a person.

I am
loved!

The New Challenge

"Brrrrr!" The alarm clock rang at exactly 6:30 a.m.—right on time—and David lay in his bed, still quite sleepy. He would've liked to sleep a little longer.

He could hear the rain outside, pounding on the windowpanes. It had been cloudy and rainy all weekend. That morning, the clouds

hung low, and a stormy wind blew through the treetops and bushes.

But David didn't mind the rain. He went for a daily walk with his dog, Buddy, no matter what the weather was like. While his four-legged friend focused on sniffing the path, David enjoyed watching the raindrops dance in the puddles. Since it was Monday, and school was restarting after the break, he couldn't linger any longer.

David quickly dressed and rushed to the kitchen. Mom was already setting the table, and David was in charge of the cereal. He hurried to say, "Good morning!" and gave his mom a kiss on the cheek. Then, he immediately started chopping fruit, which he added to the oatmeal.

"Well, David, do you feel confident about your new commute to school?" asked Mom, smiling slightly. "After all, starting today, like many other students, you will be taking the train to school by yourself!" Mom continued.

David was nine years old and in the third grade. His parents decided during the break that he was finally old enough to ride the train alone to the nearby town where his school was located.
Until now, Mom, and occasionally Dad, usually drove him to school. But that was

about to change. For Mom, it was often stressful in the mornings since David's younger siblings, Anna and Philip, needed help.

His parents had prepared David for this new challenge. Of course, he had already taken the train several times, but never alone. Recently, Mom and Dad had shown him several times what he had to pay attention to when riding the train: where to buy the ticket, which track the right train was on, how to show the conductor the ticket, and where David should get off.

He was actually a little proud that he was now allowed to ride alone, but David was a reserved and shy boy. He had a lot of friends, but he sometimes found it difficult to approach strangers. When David met

another student, he was naturally open and quickly made a friend. But approaching someone you didn't know at all? That was not easy for David, and he felt insecure about it.

David wished that Charles and Mark could also ride the train with him. They were his best friends. But Charles lived right next to the school, so he could walk. Mark lived in a nearby village and always took the bus. So, David would ride the train with only strangers. That scared him.

"Oh, Mom, can you please drive me to school one last time today? Please! It's raining!" David begged during breakfast and looked at his mom.

"No, my darling, we already discussed this yesterday. I have already bought the ticket for you! I'm sure you can do it!" Mom replied with conviction. David let out a big sigh and realized there was little point in continuing to discuss this with his mother. He realized at some point he would have to go to school on his own. Today was going to be that time. Besides, he was old enough now!

After breakfast, David said goodbye to his mom and younger siblings. He left, feeling queasy, but he managed to muster some confidence.

David walked to the train station, which was close to the apartment. Fortunately, it had stopped raining. He thought to himself that he really knew everything to look out for, after all. A little more courage arose within him, and his steps became quicker and more deliberate. To reach the station, he had to cross a busy street. A crosswalk and a traffic light eased his way. Before David crossed the street, he looked carefully to the left and right to check for cars. He had learned that from his parents.

"It's better to be safe than sorry!" his grandmother used to say.

So, to be completely sure, he looked left and right one more time and confirmed the traffic light was really on green. Everything was fine! He walked briskly across the crosswalk and reached the train station.

The station suddenly seemed larger and more intense than usual.

Many people bustled along the tracks. The sound of the arriving and departing trains drowned out the many conversations. There were women, men, and children everywhere!

Impressed by the hustle and bustle, David looked for track number four. From there, his train departed at 7:38 a.m. Right on time, it slowly rolled in and stopped with a loud hiss. David stood behind a group of passengers. An elderly gentleman opened the door by pressing a button. David cautiously climbed the stairs and looked for a good seat.

The aisles were narrow and crowded. Some people simply stood by the windows and chatted animatedly. Others were reading the newspaper or looking at their cell phones. Most of the seats were already taken. David let his gaze wander over the many rows of seats. Where should he sit? He definitely didn't want to spend the entire ride standing up. Slowly, he walked through the train car and realized he would have to ask someone if he could sit down.

Almost reaching the end of the train, David saw a boy sitting alone. He had his backpack on his lap and was staring out the window with a blank expression. David hesitated but decided to ask the boy if he could sit there. Maybe he went to the same elementary school and would be happy to meet David? "It never hurts to ask nicely!" David had once heard his grandma say.

"Good morning! Is the seat next to you still free?" asked David with a slight smile on his lips.
"Hello, yes, the seat is still free! You're welcome to sit next to me!" the boy replied, visibly pleased.
David took his backpack off his shoulders and sat down quickly because more people were pushing through the aisles behind him.

Then, he turned to the boy and said, "My name is David, by the way!" "And I'm Thomas," the boy replied.

The two smiled briefly at each other and began talking about all sorts of things. They hit it off right away and realized they had so many things in common. They went to the same school, only Thomas was already in the fourth grade. They also both enjoyed painting pictures and playing ball.

The two boys talked so eagerly that they almost forgot they had to get off the train. Together, they completed the last leg of the journey to school. David was overjoyed and convinced he had made a new friend. They even agreed to sit next to each other on the train again tomorrow.

For David, this day was a wonderful experience. The first thing he realized was that he could make his way to school completely on his own. So many concerns and fears had tormented him before. He had managed to adapt to a new and difficult environment. More importantly, he overcame his fear of approaching someone and making new friends. He learned that in life you should be open to new challenges.

David overcame his shyness, and that made him very proud. What a special and unique day!

I am brave
and strong !

The Star

Twinkle, twinkle, little star,
How I wonder what you are,
Up above the world so high,
Like a diamond in the sky.

When the blazing sun is set,
And the grass with dew is wet,
Then you show your little light,
Twinkle, twinkle, all the night.

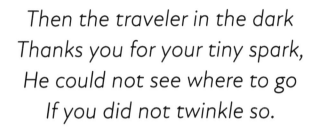

Then the traveler in the dark
Thanks you for your tiny spark,
He could not see where to go
If you did not twinkle so.

In the dark blue sky you keep,
And often through my curtains peep,
For you never shut your eye
Till the sun is in the sky.

As your bright and tiny spark
Lights the traveler in the dark,
Though I know not what you are,
Twinkle, twinkle, little star.

(by Jane Taylor)

Paul knew the whole song by heart. Satisfied with himself and the world, he closed his textbook and snuggled into his beanbag chair. His eyes wandered around the room. A little relaxation would do him some good. Tomorrow, he was supposed to sing the song "Twinkle, Twinkle, Little Star" in front of his entire music class.

Thinking about it made his stomach churn with nervousness. All of his classmates would be staring at him, and his music teacher would notice even the smallest mistake. If he suddenly forgot the lyrics, it would be so embarrassing! Paul's mom helped him learn the song by heart. Repeatedly, Paul sang the song to his mom, or he sang to himself in his bedroom. Mostly, he didn't make any mistakes. Sometimes, though, he didn't hit a note correctly, or he forgot the words. Paul always felt terrible when he messed up.

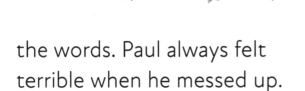

His mom comforted him every time, saying encouragingly, "Oh, Paul, don't put so much pressure on yourself. Everyone makes mistakes. Nothing and no one in the whole world is perfect."

Deep down, Paul knew his mom was right, of course. But still, he didn't want to make a mistake. He wanted to do everything perfectly, and tomorrow was his big day. After all, music was one of his favorite subjects, and he wanted to get an A on his report card like last year.

So, he practiced every day for two weeks. Of course, his mom was proud that Paul was so ambitious and could sing really well. It didn't really matter to her whether Paul got an A, B, or any other grade on his report card. The most important thing to her was that Paul was happy and didn't lose his love of singing.

It was already evening, and Paul laid down in his bed in his pajamas. He wanted to go to bed earlier than usual tonight so he could be properly rested for tomorrow. He held his music book in his hands. Once again, he read the lyrics carefully so he wouldn't forget a single line.

As she did every night, his mom came into Paul's bedroom to say goodnight before he went to bed. She knew Paul would be

performing tomorrow, and he might have trouble sleeping because of his excitement. So, Paul's mom sat down by her son's bed. She gently put her hand on Paul's shoulder and spoke softly, "Don't worry about tomorrow. You've prepared so well, and I'm sure everything will work out."

Paul slowly raised his head. Of course, he had prepared himself well. That didn't change his anxiety. At first, Paul thought about keeping his fear to himself, but then he decided to talk openly with his mom about what was bothering him. Paul was convinced it would feel good to finally talk to someone about his worries. "A sorrow shared is a sorrow halved," his mom always told him. So, Paul decided to confide in her about his feelings.

"I know I'm well-prepared, but I'm still afraid that I'll forget the lines and the other kids will laugh at me!" Paul said sadly.

His mom immediately replied, "Well, I can't imagine anyone will laugh at you. I'll let you in on a secret: The other kids are probably just as nervous as you are. That's perfectly normal and not a bad thing. Even we adults sometimes face situations where we feel very nervous. But now, you should go to sleep; otherwise, you won't be able to get out of bed tomorrow!"

His mom tenderly gave Paul a kiss on the forehead, then turned off the light and left the room.

Paul felt a little better. He was relieved and happy to have spoken with his mom.

Not long after, Paul fell asleep.

The next day, Paul packed his school supplies for class, ate a hearty breakfast, and headed off to school. In the first hour, he had English class. Normally, he always paid close attention and was very interested in the lessons. Paul liked school, but he had a hard time concentrating and staying on task that day. He was so excited and tense because he would soon be singing in front of the whole class. He couldn't think about

anything else. Luckily, he had music class next, and the wait was finally over.

After the school bell rang for second period, Paul's teacher, Mr. Richards, stood up and said to the children, "As we discussed last week, today some of you will sing the song 'Twinkle, Twinkle, Little Star.' I hope all of you have mastered the lyrics and practiced a bit at home. Who would like to come up first and perform the song?"

Immediately, the whole classroom went so quiet you could hear a pin drop. Most of the girls and boys tilted their heads down or directed their eyes out the window or to the wall. None of them wanted to start.

After about ten seconds of silence, which felt more like ten minutes to Paul, Mr. Richards continued, "All right. If none of you want to volunteer, then I'll just pick someone.
You leave me no choice!"

After this, you could feel the tension in the classroom. All the children were nervous. Paul stared at his desk. His heart began to pound faster and faster. There was no way he wanted to be the first to perform, so he repeated in his mind, "Please not me. Please not me."

Finally, Mr. Richards spoke, "Paul! Please come to the front and sing 'Twinkle, Twinkle, Little Star' for us!"

"Oh, no! Why me?" thought Paul, slightly

annoyed. Then, with knees shaking and flushed cheeks, he walked from his seat to the blackboard. The other children were visibly relieved they weren't first. Now, they all looked eagerly at Paul. He took a moment to calm himself down, taking a few deep breaths. Then, he began to sing. During the first verse, he was still nervous, and you could hear a slight tremor in his voice. Gradually, his fear started to fade. He sang the next two verses almost perfectly.

Then, it happened! A sudden halt! How did it go again? Paul had forgotten how the last stanza began. He had practiced the lyrics hundreds of times and never had a problem with the last verse. But today, of all days, in the crucial lesson in front of his teacher and all his classmates, he got stuck.

Paul's heart raced, and he looked up in despair.

Now, everyone was watching him with wide eyes. But no one laughed at him or made a rude comment—just as his mom had told him.

Mr. Richards noticed Paul was faltering and needed a little help to finish the last verse. "As your bright and tiny spark ..." Mr. Richards prompted, hoping to jog Paul's memory.

Immediately, Paul remembered. He sang the last verse from beginning to end without any mistakes. "Very nicely sung, Paul! Thank you! You may take your seat again!" said Mr. Richards, pleased.

Slowly, all the pressure lifted off Paul's shoulders, and he felt relieved. Although he hadn't sung perfectly and had even forgotten the words, he was pleased with himself. Now, it was the other children's turn, and he listened attentively.

After the lesson, he asked Mr. Richards what grade he had earned. He got a B! Paul smiled, happy with the result. How anxious he had been! He had finally done it, and no one had

laughed. Paul learned it wasn't so bad to make a mistake every once in a while.

Paul was very proud of himself for not letting his fear bring him down. Next time, it would certainly be easier for him to stand up in front of the whole class. And who knows? Maybe one day he would sing in front of a crowd at a concert. Oh, dreams are a beautiful thing.

Paul couldn't wait to tell his mom about everything. What an eventful day!

I am confident!

Closing Words

I hope you enjoyed the stories in this book. Which one was your favorite? Which story did you find the most exciting? Which story did you learn the most from?

Maybe you read this book all by yourself. That would be great! Even if your parents read the stories to you, that's perfectly fine. I'm sure you'll learn to read more fluently and quickly over the next few years. Practice makes perfect!

Hopefully, this book has shown you that you don't have to be afraid of challenges in your life. You can accomplish anything if you simply believe in yourself.

You are a great boy.
Don't forget that!

Imprint

The author is represented by: Wupi Dupi FZ-LLC
Academic Zone01-Business Center 5, RAKEZ Business Zone-FZ,
RAK, UAE
Responsible for printing: Amazon
Inspiring Stories for Amazing Boys
Amelia Kinsley

ISBN: 9798345297193
Second edition 2024
© 2024 Amelia Kinsley

Made in the USA
Las Vegas, NV
24 November 2024

12518970R10060